THE SILLIEST SCHOOL JOKE BOOK EVER!

AMANDA LI

Illustrated by
JOHN KELLY

PUFFIN

*To Isabelle, and all her friends at Wimbledon Park School,
not forgetting top joke-tellers, Louis and Luke.*

PUFFIN BOOKS

Published by the Penguin Group
Penguin Books Ltd, 80 Strand, London WC2R 0RL, England
Penguin Group (USA) Inc., 375 Hudson Street, New York, New York 10014, USA
Penguin Group (Canada), 10 Alcorn Avenue, Toronto, Ontario, Canada M4V 3B2
(a division of Pearson Penguin Canada Inc.)
Penguin Ireland, 25 St Stephen's Green, Dublin 2, Ireland (a division of Penguin Books Ltd)
Penguin Group (Australia), 250 Camberwell Road, Camberwell, Victoria 3124, Australia
(a division of Pearson Australia Group Pty Ltd)
Penguin Books India Pvt Ltd, 11 Community Centre, Panchsheel Park,
New Delhi – 110 017, India
Penguin Group (NZ), cnr Airborne and Rosedale Roads, Albany, Auckland 1310,
New Zealand (a division of Pearson New Zealand Ltd)
Penguin Books (South Africa) (Pty) Ltd, 24 Sturdee Avenue, Rosebank,
Johannesburg 2196, South Africa

Penguin Books Ltd, Registered Offices: 80 Strand, London WC2R 0RL, England

www.penguin.com

First published 2005
1

Text copyright © Puffin Books, 2005
Illustrations copyright © John Kelly, 2005
All rights reserved

The moral right of the illustrator has been asserted

Designed by Cathy Tincknell
Made and printed in England by Clays Ltd, St Ives plc

British Library Cataloguing in Publication Data
A CIP catalogue record for this book is available from the British Library

ISBN 0–141–31939–9

CONTENTS

INTRODUCTION

School, eh? It's a funny old place, isn't it? Well, ok, it's not **that** funny, especially when they do things like spring a surprise test on you or give you **tons** of extra homework — but we've just the thing to change all that. This **super-silly** joke book will brighten up those long boring days until the next school holidays come. You'll find **hundreds of jokes** on every bit of school life, from ludicrous lunchboxes to terrible school trips. So put some **chuckles** into your classroom and get reading!

TERRIBLE TEACHERS

WITH TEACHERS LIKE THESE, WHO NEEDS ENEMIES?

What's the difference between a teacher and a wild pig?
None - they're both a bit of a boar.

Why did the teacher wear sunglasses to school?
Because her class were too bright for her.

Why is the pottery class so quiet?
The teacher threatened to kiln them.

R.I.P.

What did one computer teacher say to the other?
'It's all geek to me.'

Why is a teacher like a hiker? They both ramble on.

Pupil: I'm doing a project on mountains.

Teacher: You'd better get on top of it, then.

Why did the bald teacher draw rabbits on his head? He thought they would look like hares from a distance.

What do ghostly teachers give their pupils to do? Moanwork.

What's a maths teacher's favourite creature?
An adder.

What's the maths teacher's favourite instrument?
The triangle.

What's a history teacher's favourite snack?
Dates.

Teacher: Lucy, where is your MUM FROM?
Lucy: ALaska.
Teacher: Don't bother, I'LL ask her myself.

What do you call a well-educated person who shouts at kids the whole time?
A teacher.

PUPIL: I'm doing a project on weights and measures.
Teacher: Is it heavy-going?

PUPIL: My project is on rock climbing.
Teacher: You really should get to grips with it.

Teacher: Spell the word 'weather'.

Pupil: Erm, W-E-V-A-R.

Teacher: That's the worst spell of weather we've ever had.

Why did the teacher turn the light off? Because his class was so dim.

There's Good News and There's Bad News . . .

QUIETEN DOWN, YOU NOISY LOT! THE HEADMISTRESS IS TRYING TO TELL US SOME **VERY** IMPORTANT NEWS . . .

THE GOOD NEWS IS . . .
The school is being closed down for a month.

THE BAD NEWS IS . . .
We've found an alternative location – 'Brats' Camp: the academy that whips misbehaving little monsters into shape.'

THE GOOD NEWS IS . . .
The school canteen is being improved.
THE BAD NEWS IS . . .
It's having a new roof. The food stays the same.

THE GOOD NEWS IS . . .
The playground is being extended.
THE BAD NEWS IS . . .
We'll be building a brand-new examination hall in the extra space.

THE GOOD NEWS IS . . .
Our school is going to be on TV.
THE BAD NEWS IS . . .
It's on a documentary about the worst-performing schools in the country.

PIE

SCHOOL FROM HELL!

THE GOOD NEWS IS . . .
Mr Grimshaw (the school's most unpopular teacher) will be off sick for at least two months.

THE BAD NEWS IS . . .
He's got a very itchy and highly contagious skin disease that he may have passed on to the entire school before he left.

THE GOOD NEWS IS . . .

A celebrity is coming to visit our school.

THE BAD NEWS IS . . .
It's the local mayor.

THE GOOD NEWS IS . . .
We'll be having a school disco next month.
THE BAD NEWS IS . . .
Mr Bland the music teacher will be demonstrating his version of 'rapping' and 'break-dancing'.

THE GOOD NEWS IS . . .
Pupils will no longer be required to do 'homework'.
THE BAD NEWS IS . . .
We'll be re-naming it 'evening work', 'weekend work' and 'any spare moment you've got work'.

ASK A TEACHER . . .

GOT A PROBLEM? WHY NOT ASK A HELPFUL
TEACHER? WELL, HERE'S
WHY NOT . . .

'Teacher,
Teacher, my
pen's run out.'
'Well, go and
chase after it,
then.'

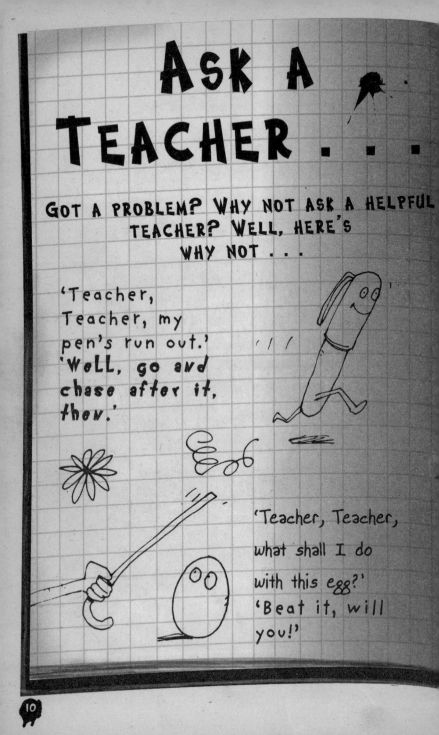

'Teacher, Teacher,
what shall I do
with this egg?'
'Beat it, will
you!'

'Teacher, Teacher, a dog just bit me.'
'I'll give you some cream for it.'
'But it's just run off!'

'Teacher, Teacher, everyone keeps disagreeing with me.'
'Of course they don't.'

'Teacher, Teacher, I've just swallowed my recorder!'
'Aren't you glad you don't play the piano?'

'Teacher, Teacher, no one takes me seriously.'
'Oh, stop being ridiculous.'

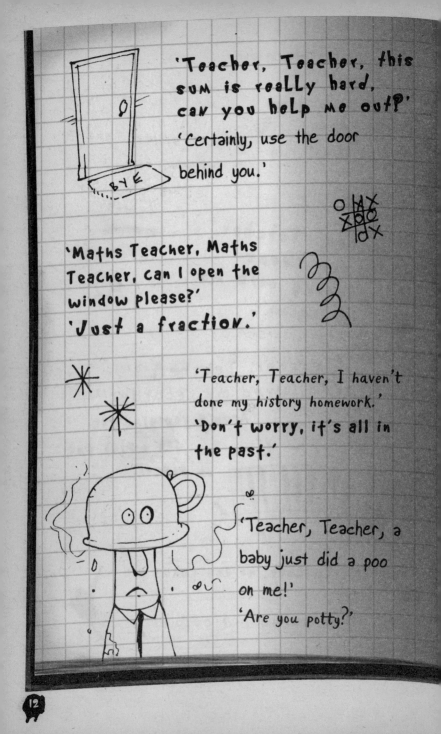

'Teacher, Teacher, this sum is really hard, can you help me out?'

'Certainly, use the door behind you.'

'Maths Teacher, Maths Teacher, can I open the window please?'

'Just a fraction.'

'Teacher, Teacher, I haven't done my history homework.'

'Don't worry, it's all in the past.'

'Teacher, Teacher, a baby just did a poo on me!'

'Are you potty?'

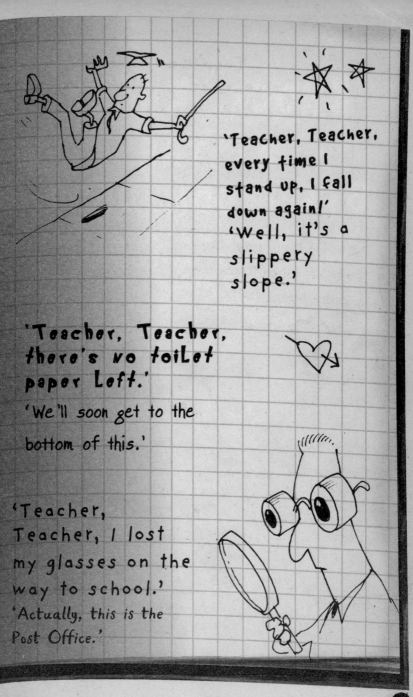

'Teacher, Teacher, every time I stand up, I fall down again!'
'Well, it's a slippery slope.'

'Teacher, Teacher, there's no toilet paper left.'
'We'll soon get to the bottom of this.'

'Teacher, Teacher, I lost my glasses on the way to school.'
'Actually, this is the Post Office.'

'KNOCK, KNOCK'
AT THE
STAFFROOM DOOR

WANT TO KNOW WHAT GOES ON IN
THE TEACHERS' SACRED ROOM?
READ ON . . .

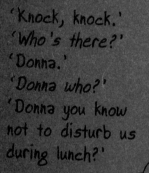

'Knock, knock.'
'Who's there?'
'Donna.'
'Donna who?'
'Donna you know
not to disturb us
during lunch?'

'Knock, knock.'
'Who's there?'
'Harry.'
'Harry who?'
'Harry up with that
cuppa, would you?'

'Knock, knock.'
'Who's there?'
'Meg.'
'Meg who?'
'Meg us another cup
of tea, would you?'

'Knock, knock.'
'Who's there?'
'Sam.'
'Sam who?'
'Sam more biscuits, please.'

'Knock, knock.'
'Who's there?'
'Anna.'
'Anna who?'
'Anna'ther class of no-hopers to teach
this term . . .'

'Knock, knock.'
'Who's there?'
'Justin.'
'Justin who?'
'Ooh, justin time for
another coffee.'

BARMY BOOKS

Eating Crisps at the Back of the Class BY RUSSELL LOUDLEE

HOW TO LOSE YOUR CLASS ON A SCHOOL TRIP BY WANDA OFF

The Naughtiest Pupil in the Class by Hope Lesscase

WANT TO TRAIN AS A TEACHER? BY R. U. INSANE

MAKE MONEY AT THE SCHOOL FÊTE by Tom Bola

School Lunches by Dean R. Bell

PASSING YOUR SATS by Anne Sirs

COMMON SPELLING ERRORS by Miss Take

TELLING OFF THE INDIVIDUAL BY C. ME LATER

TEACHERS AT THE SCHOOL DISCO by Dan Sinbadly

TOP TEN EXCUSES FOR BEING LATE FOR SCHOOL

1. I squeezed the toothpaste too hard and it took me half an hour to get it all back in.

2. My parents locked me in the cellar and then forgot I was there.

3. I was abducted by extra-terrestrials.

4. I was doing early morning training for the Olympic synchronized swimming squad.

5. My watch is slow and my parents are too mean to buy me a new battery.

6. I had an important video to watch.

7. Breakfast time at our house is so stressful that I needed to take a relaxing walk before school.

8. I choked on the free gift in the cereal packet and had to be resuscitated.

9. The car broke down. I know I only live round the corner but it was blocking my way.

10. I don't actually know what time school starts as I've never got here on time before.

LOONY LUNCHBOXES

WHAT'S LURKING IN YOURS? SNACKS THAT ARE YUMMY OR JUST VERY CRUMMY?

What did the pupil say to the carrot?
'It's been nice gnawing you.'

Why did the sandwich go to the dentist?
It needed a filling.

What did the loaf say to the knife?
'Can I get a slice of the action?'

What did the slice of
bread say to the knife?
'Are you buttering me up?'

What did one jam
sandwich say to the
other?
'We're in a
very sticky
situation.'

What did one cheese sandwich
say to the other?
'We've got ourselves
into a pickle.'

What did the egg say
when it saw the bread
and butter?
Nothing. It wouldn't come
out of its shell.

What do you get if you
have two bananas in your lunchbox?

A pair of slippers.

What did one banana

say to the other?
'You really apeel to me.'

What do you get if you cross
a banana with a con-man?
A very slippery customer.

What did the
boy apple
say when he
saw the
gorgeous girl
apple?
'Core!'

What did one bunch of grapes
say to the other?
'I'm feeling vine.'

What did the
under-ripe tomato
say to the over-
ripe tomato?
'Oooh, you've gone
all red!'

What's hot and spicy and
happens after school?
Extra curry-icular activities.

What snack
can you find
in space?
Astro-nuts.

DONG

DONG Who can eat crisps
and ring bells at the
same time?
The Crunchback of Notre-Dame.

What are goldfishes'
favourite crisps?
Salt and fin-egar.

**Which biscuits
have Lots of
pocket-money?**
Rich Tea.

What did the mummy
sultana say to the
daddy sultana?
'Raisin kids is hard.'

Which biscuits race round
and crash into each other?
Jammie Dodgems.

Which biscuits
drone on and on
about themselves?
Bore-bons.

TOP TEN THINGS
YOU DON'T WANT TO FIND
IN YOUR LUNCHBOX

1. A manky banana that dissolves into brown gloop as it's peeled.

2. Last night's cold pasta, masquerading as 'salad'.

3. A deadly virus that could unleash a worldwide epidemic.

4. A selection of plastic cheese slices from your little sister's toy food set.

5. Anything with 'use by 2001' printed on it.

6. Sneeze 'n' onion crisps — the exciting new flavour.

7. A Teletubbies yoghurt (awww, sweet . . .)

8. Raw sewage.

9. A Choco-mocko bar — the new sugar-free, low fat, healthy alternative to chocolate.

10. Any sandwiches made by your mum.

BAD, BAD BOYS AND GIRLS

THESE PAINFUL PUPILS ARE REALLY PUSHING THEIR LUCK . . .

Teacher: Jack, I hope I didn't see you kicking Luke just then.
Jack: I hope you didn't, either.

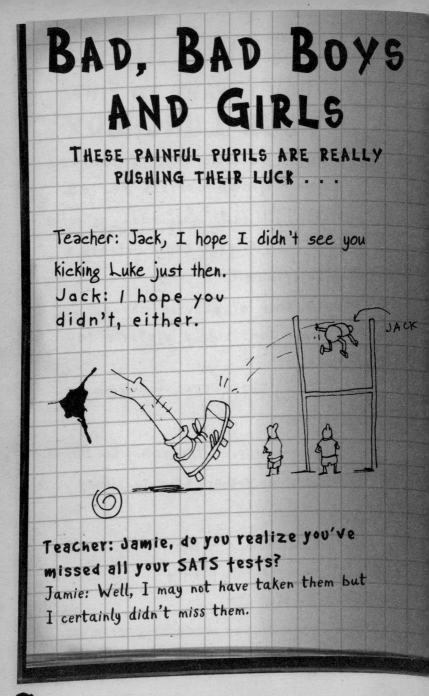

Teacher: Jamie, do you realize you've missed all your SATS tests?
Jamie: Well, I may not have taken them but I certainly didn't miss them.

Science teacher: What's the difference between electricity and lightning?

Smartypants: You don't have to pay for lightning.

English teacher: What word is always spelt incorrectly?
Smartypants: 'Incorrectly.'

Teacher: Name the four food groups.
Pupil: Erm, fast, junk, frozen and tinned.

Teacher: Sam, have you been copying your homework from the internet?

Sam: No, sir, my dad never goes online.

WWW. CHEAT. COM

Teacher: What's the outside of a tree called, Adam?

Adam: I don't know.

Teacher: Bark, Adam, bark!

Adam: Woof, woof.

Woof!
Woof!

Teacher: What's the capital of France?

Pupil: Erm, F?

Pupil: Mum, the teacher shouted at me today for something I didn't do.

Mother: What was that?

Pupil: My homework.

Teacher: Your homework's improved lately.

Pupil: Yes, my dad's stopped helping me.

← DAD

ME

NAUGHTY
'KNOCK, KNOCKS'

'Knock, knock.'
'Who's there?'
'Lego.'
'Lego who?'
'Lego of me, you
big bully!'

'Knock, knock.'
'Who's there?'
'Ida.'
'Ida who?'
'Ida know the
answer, do you?'

'Knock, knock.'
'Who's there?'
'Vanna.'
'Vanna who?'
'Vanna bunk off school?'

'Knock, knock.'
'Who's there?'
'Luke.'
'Luke who?'
'Luke out, here comes
the headmaster!'

'Knock, knock.'
'Who's there?'
'Heavy.'
'Heavy who?'
'Heavy ever been
suspended?'

EVEN BARMIER

WHEN TO REPAIR YOUR SCHOOL
BY RUFUS FALLING

What to Wear on Wet School Trips by Anna Rak

THE WELCOMING HEADMASTER by Doris Open

Great Unanswered Questions
BY HOWARD I. KNOW

DOING SUMS by Kenny Ad

BOOKS . . . .

WRITING SICK NOTES by Abby Sent

TAKING YOUR CLASS TO A FOREST by Lucinda Woods

FINISH THAT TEST by Gladys Over

FINISHING A BOOK by N. Dex

SUPPLYING SCHOOL TOILETS BY ANN DREX

SILLY SCHOOL
PETS

EVERY SCHOOL NEEDS A PET — BUT
PETS CERTAINLY DON'T NEED AWFUL
JOKES LIKE THESE . . .

What do you call an
angry school pet?
A grrrr-bil.

Why was the rabbit
Looking grumpy?
He was having a bad
hare day.

What did one rabbit say
to the other rabbit?
'Ear-sy come, ear-sy go.'

What did one hamster say to the other? 'I'm having a wheel good time.'

What should you do if the school pet gets sick? Give it mouse-to-mouse resuscitation.

What you call the school pet on a diet? A skinny-pig.

What do you call a happy school pet? A grinny-pig.

Why do mice, hamsters and guinea-pigs all love boats? Because they're row-dents.

Why do mice tell each other stories? Because they've all got tails to tell.

How do fish always start their stories? Once a pond a time . . .

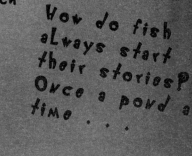

What's the goldfishes' favourite story? Finderella.

Does the school cat really know how to use the video? No, it can only press paws.

NUTTY KNOWLEDGE

RIGHT, START TAKING NOTES AND CATCH UP. WE'RE WAY BEHIND WITH OUR SERIOUSLY SILLY STUDYING.

Why did the English teacher bring a knife to class?
She wanted to spread the word.

What do you get if you cross loud music with an English lesson?
Punktuation.

Why is English class like going to jail?
You know you're in for a long sentence.

English teacher: Can anyone give me a sentence using the word 'climate'?

Pupil: The mountain was so high I couldn't climate.

English teacher: Can anyone give me a sentence using the word 'column'?

Pupil: I column my friends on my mobile.

English teacher: Can anyone give me a sentence using the word 'diploma'?

Pupil: When your pipes are leaking, call diploma.

Why did the drama teacher tell his class off?
They were acting up.

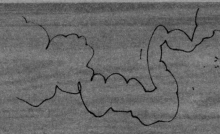

What do you call the lesson where you get to watch Star Trek for the whole hour?
Sci-fi-ence.

What do you get if you cross the music class with the science class?
A test tuba.

What do you get when you cross P.E. with assembly?
Hymn-nastics.

Who's married to the geography teacher's uncle?
Aunt Arctica.

What's a glacier's favourite song?
'Freeze a jolly good fellow . . .'

What do you call a sea
that's always on a diet?
The Thindian Ocean.

Which mountain is always on the go?
Mount Never-rest.

What's big, cold and really
stupid?
An ice-berk.

What tool does
the maths
teacher use?
Multi-pliers.

What do you call a
maths teacher who
can do tricks?
A mathemagician.

What do you call a sea that eats a lot?
The Fatlantic.

Were the pyramids built by the Egyptians?
I sphinx so.

What does the maths class have instead of desks?
Times tables.

Why was the river so relaxed?
It just went with the flow.

Why was the class so bad at decimal numbers?

They couldn't see the point.

How do you calm down a baby on a spaceship?
Rocket.

What have a calculator and a reliable friend got in common?

You can count on them.

How does the moon cut its hair?
Eclipse it.

Why did the wind blow so fast?
It was a hurry-cane.

DISGUSTING JOKE CORNER

ANY PUPILS OF A SENSITIVE NATURE, PLEASE LEAVE THE CLASSROOM NOW . . .

Who's good at drawing but has terrible wind? The fart teacher.

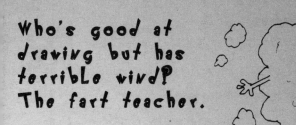

Where does Windy Wayne, the smelliest schoolboy in the world, live? In a flat-ulent.

Mandy: I sneezed all over the headmaster yesterday.

Andy: How is he?

Mandy: Snot too happy.

Did you hear the one about the nose at the school disco? It wanted to get down and bogie.

What did the nose shout out at the school play auditions? 'Pick me, pick me!'

Did you hear the one about the schoolboy who came out of the toilets smiling? He was flushed with success.

What sits on the toilet and logs on? The school com-poo-ter.

What did the toilet paper say to the pupil? 'You tear me apart.'

What's the best instrument to play in the school toilets?
The pee-ano.

What's the best song to sing while you're on the toilet?
'Wee are the Champions.'

Which subject is best at burping?
History, because it's always repeating itself.

What's the best game to play in the school toilets?
Plopscotch.

What do you call the smelliest person at school?
A phew-pil.

PARENT POWER

IMAGINE WHAT IT MUST BE LIKE BEING IN A FAMILY OF SUPERHEROES... (IN YOUR DREAMS! — ED.) WHAT WOULD THE TEACHER SAY ON PARENTS' EVENING?

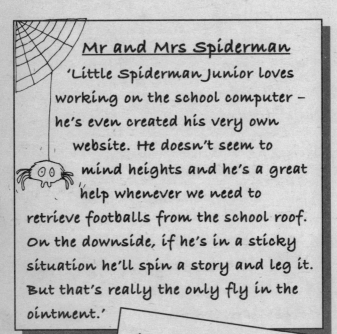

Mr and Mrs Spiderman

'Little Spiderman Junior loves working on the school computer — he's even created his very own website. He doesn't seem to mind heights and he's a great help whenever we need to retrieve footballs from the school roof. On the downside, if he's in a sticky situation he'll spin a story and leg it. But that's really the only fly in the ointment.'

Mr and Mrs Wolverine

'Little Wolfie is a popular boy who gets his teeth into every subject. He'll go fur.'

Mr and Mrs Catwoman

'A delight! Kitty is a mewsical child who loves DJing (they tell me she's very good at mixing and scratching). We're a little concerned about the dead mouse she presented to her class teacher, but other than that we find her a complete purrfectionist.'

Mr and Mrs Superman

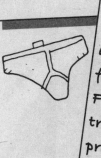

'Superman Junior may be faster than a speeding bullet but he's always late for my classes. Needs improvement! Furthermore, he isn't sticking to the traditional school uniform – we do prefer underpants to be worn on the INSIDE of the trousers.'

Mr and Mrs Incredible Hulk

'Very jealous of his classmates – at times, we've seen him green with envy. He must learn to control his temper. Also, his school uniform is looking rather tattered – perhaps a trip to the shops is due?'

DISGUSTING SCHOOL DINNERS

IN THE SCHOOL CANTEEN, WE ALL KNOW THAT WHAT GOES DOWN, MUST COME UP . . .

You know your school canteen's really terrible when:

The mice are using the custard as a trampoline.

You break a tooth on the jelly.

The food's so cold, even the potatoes have got their jackets on.

The gravy is served by the slice.

Instead of a knife and fork you get a hammer and chisel.

You eat a school lunch if you want the next day off school.

The meat is so tough it stands up and asks you for a fight.

You catch the school cook phoning for a pizza.

What's the difference between school dinners and a pile of poo? School dinners come on a plate.

What did the fish say to the chips? 'Come over to my plaice.'

Dinner Lady: Any seconds?
Pupil: No thanks, I'm too young to die.

What goes 'Yuk,' bump, 'Yuk,' bump, 'Yuk,' bump, 'Yuk,' bump . . .?
A hall full of pupils tasting their school dinner and fainting.

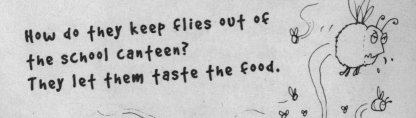

How do they keep flies out of the school canteen?
They let them taste the food.

Why were the police looking for a tin of beans?
They were faked beans.

BEANS

FAKED BEANS

Why were the police looking for a green bean?
It was doing a runner.

What do you get if you cross school vegetables with a necklace?
A food chain.

What do you get when you cross a pasta dish with a bhangra beat?
Spaghetti Bolly-naise.

What do you get when you cross a dog with school vegetables? A collie-flower.

Why was the hot dog so pleased with itself? It was on a roll.

Why was the vegetable sitting on its own? It wanted some peas and quiet.

What did one piece of pasta say to the other? 'A penne for your thoughts.'

What sits in a dish and trembles?
Cowardly Custard.

Why did the ice cream get told off?
The headmistress couldn't cone-done its behaviour.

What do school chips and the history class have in common?
Ancient Grease.

What happened to the boy who drank eight cans of coke?
He brought 7 up.

TRULY AWFUL TRIPS

WHETHER IT'S A DAY OUT OR A WHOLE WEEK AWAY, THE BEST BIT ABOUT SCHOOL TRIPS IS COMING HOME AT THE END.

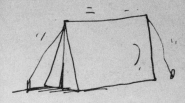

How do you stop yourself getting lost in the woods?
Stay in your tent.

What did the class write on at the beach?
Sandpaper.

Why did the teacher storm off during the rock climbing?
He was at the end of his tether.

Who invented the school coach? I don't know but it was a wheely good idea.

What did the bossy teacher do on the trip to the zoo?
He made his class lion up.

Why did the teacher shout at his class on the zoo trip?
Because they were monkeying around.

Why did the teacher
shout at his class on
the farm trip?
Because they were
mucking about.

Why did the teacher tell
his class to shut up on
the farm trip?
They were shouting at
each udder.

What zips up the side and
shows off all night?
A sleeping brag.

What did the top bed say
to the bottom bed?
'Let's bunk off!'

Why does no one ever laugh on the school skiing trip? Snow joke.

Where's the best place to buy candy? Sweetzerland.

What did the ski teacher say to his class? 'Avalanche now or you'll be hungry later.'

What do you get when a bunch of beginner skiers stay at your house for the night? A slipover.

Where's the best place to go fishing? Finland.

Where's the best place for the music class to visit? Singapore.

Where's the best place to go if you want fried food? Greece.

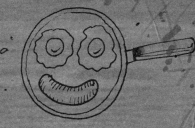

Which creature loves camping? An octopus, because he's got lots of tent-acles.

Where's the best place to go if you haven't got much time? Russia.

YOU KNOW YOU'RE ON A
SCHOOL TRIP
WHEN . . .

A bunch of kids are making a dash for the back of the coach to make stupid faces at the cars following behind.

You've eaten your entire packed lunch within five minutes of the coach leaving.

You've been sick all over the seat within ten minutes of the coach leaving.

Some kid is homesick and crying for his mummy - and the coach hasn't even left the school car park yet.

Someone wanders off on the field trip, raising a full-scale alarm and search party. He's eventually found lying casually on his bunk, reading.

RESCUE

Someone starts telling spooky stories after Lights out and gives everyone nightmares.

You have to fill in lots of questionnaires about everything you've seen. Lots and lots of them. In fact, you have to fill in a questionnaire about all the other questionnaires you did on the trip.

GEOGRAPHY
'KNOCK, KNOCKS'
WHERE IN THE WORLD DID WE FIND JOKES LIKE THESE?

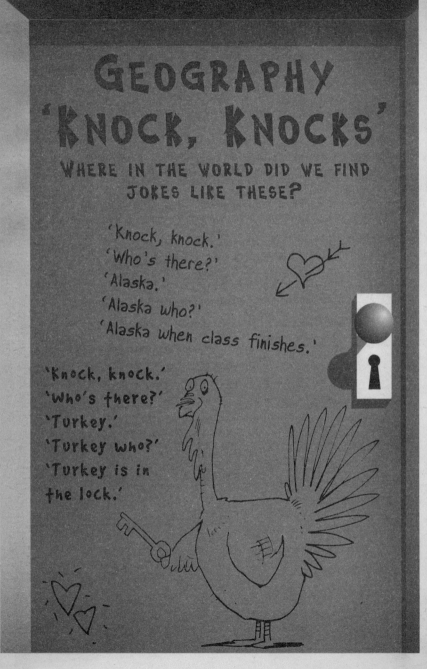

'Knock, knock.'
'Who's there?'
'Alaska.'
'Alaska who?'
'Alaska when class finishes.'

'Knock, knock.'
'Who's there?'
'Turkey.'
'Turkey who?'
'Turkey is in the lock.'

'Knock, knock.'
'Who's there?'
'Everest.'
'Everest who?'
'Everest your eyes during a boring class?'

'Knock, knock.'
'Who's there?'
'Arctic.'
'Arctic who?'
'Arctic'll you, if you don't tell me your secret!'

'Knock, knock.'
'Who's there?'
'India.'
'India who?'
'India yourself and you have to go to hospital.'

'Knock, knock.'
'Who's there?'
'India.'
'India who?'
'India afternoon, I'm going to the dentist.'

'Knock, knock.'
'Who's there?'
'Kenya.'
'Kenya who?'
'Kenya keep the noise down, please?'

'Knock, knock.'
'Who's there?'
'Jamaica.'
'Jamaica who?'
'Jamaica come to the school play?'

'Knock, knock.'
'Who's there?'
'Arizona.'
'Arizona who?'
'Arizona so many times I will knock on this door!'

POTTY PARENTS

SOME PARENTS ARE NEVER HAPPY. SO SOME HEAD TEACHERS HAVE TO DEAL WITH LUDICROUS LETTERS LIKE THESE.

Dear Head

We'd like to ask why our son is being denied 24-hour access to the school computer. Apart from improving his IT skills, if he doesn't get the internet shopping done, we'll have nothing for tea tomorrow.

Yours truly

Mrs Webb

Dear Head

We think that Adam is getting far too much homework. It's causing a lot of stress, especially those really hard sums that we can't work out.

Yours sincerely

Mr and Mrs Upp

Dear Head

We're very disappointed that our daughter isn't playing the most important part in the nativity play this year. We've spent a lot of money on extra drama classes for her and we really think she can do better than playing the sheep. It's woolly thinking on your part.

Yours obnoxiously

Mr and Mrs Pushyparent

Dear Head

We'd like to ask permission to take a three-week holiday during term time. Of course, we won't be taking the children with us but can they sleep over at school while we're away? We don't want the house to get trashed.

Yours affectionately

Mr and Mrs Houseproud

Dear Head

I'm writing to complain about the school sponsored walk that took place last Saturday. Surely proper maps could have been given to the children? It's now Wednesday and little William still hasn't found his way home.

Yours patiently

Mr and Mrs Waite

U R LOST

CRAZY CLUBS

THESE EXTRA-CURRICULAR ACTIVITIES ARE EXCRUCIATING!

Why is the breakfast club
like a pig's tail?
They're both twirly.

Why does everyone want
to go to breakfast club?
Cereal laugh.

Why did the
pupils stop
going to
computer
club?
They lost
their drive.

Why is there no
gymnastics club in
winter?
They're into
summersaults.

What does the chess
club have for snacks?
Pawn sandwiches.

Why does the
French club always
need the loo?
They go 'Oui, oui'
all the time.

What did the French
club say when they
saw their school
dinner?
'Mercy!'

Why did the
tennis club
get told off?
They were
making a
racket.

Why was the games club cancelled?
There were too many draughts in the room.

Where is the Spanish club today?
They're on olé-day.
Why is the eco-club always lying down?
They're trying to save energy.

Why is the swimming club like the school cat?
They both like their strokes.

Why is the cookery club really cruel?
They love beating and whipping.

'KNOCK, KNOCK,'
GET A TELLING OFF!

'Knock, knock.'
'Who's there?'
'Ketchup.'
'Ketchup who?'
'Ketchup on your homework!'

'Knock, knock.'
'Who's there?'
'Plane.'
'Plane who?'
'Plane dumb won't help you now!'

'Knock, knock.'
'Who's there?'
'Lionel.'
'Lionel who?'
'Lionel get you nowhere,
young lady!'

'Knock, knock.'
'Who's there?'
'Europe.'
'Europe who?'
'Europe to no good again, boy!'

'Knock, knock.'
'Who's there?'
'Arena.'
'Arena who?'
'You arena lot of
trouble!'

UNUSUAL CLASSROOM CREATURES

THESE PETS COME FROM ALL OVER THE WORLD — AND THESE JOKES ARE OUT OF THIS WORLD.

What do bald stick insects wear on their heads?
T-wigs.

Why couldn't the stick insect get to the bank? They'd closed down his branch.

What do you call a baby stick insect?
A Twiglet.

What do you get if you cross a lizard with a famous scientist?
Newt-on.

What did one stick insect say to the other?
'Leaf me alone.'

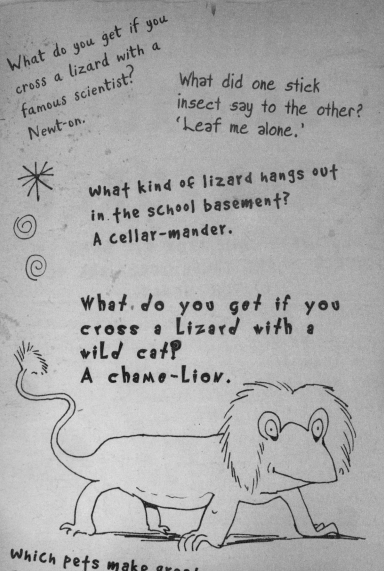

What kind of lizard hangs out in the school basement?
A cellar-mander.

What do you get if you cross a Lizard with a wild cat?
A chame-Lion.

Which pets make great secret agents?
Spyders.

What do frogs play in the playground? Hopscotch.

What do frogs wear in the summer?

Open-toad sandals.

How deep should the frog pond be? Kneedeep, kneedeep, kneedeep.

What did one frog say to the other? 'That's toad-ally awesome.'

What sort of creature is a slug? A snail with a housing problem.

THE LIBRARY OF LAUGHS

WELCOME, BOOKWORMS, TO THE BARMY
BOOK CORNER, WHERE YOU CAN FIND A
LOAD OF DUSTY OLD JOKES LURKING AT
THE BACK OF THE SHELVES.

What goes 'Cluck' and is
found in a library?
A hen-cyclopedia.

Where do jungle
animals find their
books?
In a lion-brary.

EGGLAYING
FOR
EXPERTS

Which famous writer goes best with a hot dog?
Roll Dahl.

Which famous Victorian author was a bit slow on the uptake?
Charles Thickens.

What happened when a skunk wrote a book about his life?
It became a best-smeller.

On which day do criminals read a lot?
World Crook Day.

Why did the book change its colour? It wanted to be read.

What did one library book say to the other? 'Can I take you out?'

What stories do cats like best? Furry tails.

Why are books like spies? They're both undercover.

How do you know if a book is going out? It puts on its best jacket.

Why was the book upset?
It was left on the shelf.

What rhymes and
is found in the
school toilet?
A poo-em.

Why was the writer
confused?
She'd lost the plot.

What did one book
say to the other?
'Page me.'

What makes some
books scary?
Shivers running
down their spines.

TRULY AWFUL

Fractions Are Not the Only Way
BY DES E. MALS

HOW TO DRAW PERFECTLY by Trace de Picture

BETTER BACKFLIPS BY JIM NASTICS

HOW TO CHEAT IN TESTS by P. King

FOOTBALL FOR BEGINNERS by Owen Goal

TEXTBOOKS

IMPORTANT FACTS ABOUT FORESTS by Teresa Green

READING MAPS BY DI REKSHUNS

MAKING AN IMPACT IN SCIENCE BY N. X. PLOSION

GEOMETRICAL SHAPES by Sir Cumference

How to Paint Brilliant Pictures by Mick L. Angelo

FAMOUS FACES

THROUGHOUT HISTORY, PEOPLE HAVE ACHIEVED GREAT THINGS. THESE JOKES AREN'T SOME OF THEM . . .

When did Henry the Eighth die? Just a few days before they buried him.

Who was the scariest nurse in history? Florence Frightingale.

Which famous French commander always wet himself?
Nappy-oleon.

Which king had a noisy bottom? Richard the Lionfart.

What do you get if you cross a famous warrior with a fruit?
Alexander the Grape.

Which Royals ate
a lot of meat?
The Eliza-beef-ans

Which queen was the
best at scoring goals?
Anne, because she
got the Boleyn.

Which queen burped a lot?
Queen Hic-toria.

Which Egyptian
queen was
always in the
bath?
Clean-opatra.

Why was King Arthur always tired?
He had a lot of sleepless knights.

z z z z z z z z z

Which royals ate a Lot of gum?
The Chew-dors.

Who was the smelliest person to invade Britain?
William the Pong-queror.

What did the Romans say when it rained?
'Hail, Caesar.'

Which hero had terrible spots? The Scarlet Pimple-nel.

Where did King Arthur study? At Knight school.

Which famous painting never stops complaining? The Moaner Lisa.

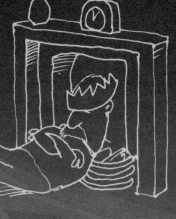

Which king always slept in the fireplace? Alfred the Grate.

82

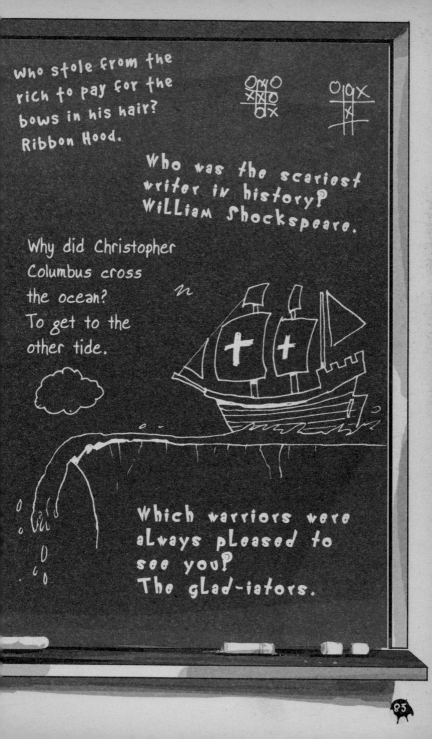

Who stole from the rich to pay for the bows in his hair?
Ribbon Hood.

Who was the scariest writer in history?
William Shockspeare.

Why did Christopher Columbus cross the ocean?
To get to the other tide.

Which warriors were always pleased to see you?
The glad-iators.

83

YOU KNOW ALIENS HAVE TAKEN OVER THE BODIES OF EVERYONE AT YOUR SCHOOL WHEN . . .

There's a whopping great flying saucer in the middle of the playground.

ALL the pupils are acting really strangely: so well-behaved and quiet.

During assembly, the headmaster scratches his neck and you notice he's wearing a stick-on 'headmaster' face.

The school secretary smiles at you and asks how you are.

When you accidentally spill a glass of water on your classmate's hand, it sizzles, then melts.

You're beamed up to a waiting spaceship so that the alien teacher can use you to demonstrate its 'What is a human?' biology class.

HUMAN

Your teacher gives you top marks for everything you do, all day.

At lunchtime, everything gets eaten — including the knives, forks, glasses and trays.

THE JOKER'S GUIDE TO THE SCHOOL FÊTE

HURRAH! IT'S THE ANNUAL SCHOOL FÊTE! THIS YEAR, WHY NOT MAKE THE PROCEEDINGS A LITTLE MORE EXCITING WITH OUR GREAT IDEAS FOR PRACTICAL JOKES?

Trick 1 — Bouncy, bouncy . . .

Is it possible to fly without wings? Well, now it can be. Find some heavy weights. Attach them securely round your waist, then jump into the middle of the bouncy castle. Watch in wonder as everyone else flies

approximately 30 metres up into the air.

Trick 2 - The Not-So-Lucky Dip

Turn the lucky dip into a mucky dip by pouring 30 litres of guacamole into the tub. Sit back and watch people's faces as they pull out their slimy, green, dripping hands. Sneeze loudly for extra effect

LUCKY

DIP

Trick 3 - Spice it up!

'Help out' at the burger stand by mixing a jar of chilli powder into the tomato ketchup and pouring it back into the bottle. Red faces all round. School days have never been so hot, hot, hot!

Trick 4 – It's priceLess!

Volunteer for the bric-a-brac stall. Liven up the proceedings (and get loads of cash for a pile of old rubbish) by adding a few extra noughts and pound signs to the prices. Lo and behold, that manky old lampshade selling for 20p is now a sought-after antique retailing at £200. Eat your heart out, Antiques Roadshow!

£200

GIANTS TEA CUP.

STUPID SCHOOL SPORTS DAY

It's time to show off your amazing athletic abilities and get really competitive. Either that or have a nice sit down and watch everyone else making a complete fool of themselves. Whatever you do, don't forget to listen out for some very important announcements.

'Hello, everyone, and welcome to our annual sports day. Before the fun begins, we're sorry to say that the three-legged race will be slightly delayed. The competitors are all a bit tied up at the moment.'

'Any help setting up the egg-and-spoon race would be much appreciated. We'd like to crack on as soon as possible.'

'Thanks to everyone who volunteered to assist in the sack race. People have been falling over themselves to help out.'

'Entrants to the parents' race, please gather at the starting point. After last year's fiasco, please note that there is to be no spitting, swearing or fighting. And that goes for you too, Headmaster.'

'If anyone else wishes to compete in the hurdles, there will be no obstacles put in your way.'

91

SPORTING ANTICS

IT'S NOT ABOUT WINNING, IT'S ABOUT TAKING PART. BUT IF YOU DON'T WIN ALL YOUR MATCHES THIS TERM, THE HEADMASTER WILL BE AFTER YOUR TEAM WITH A BASEBALL BAT. (HE'S A LOVELY MAN REALLY . . .)

Why is the hockey pitch all wet? The team's been practising their dribbling.

How do you know when the captain of the cricket team loses his temper?
He stumps his foot.

Why is the cricket team having a meeting?
They're just batting a few ideas around.

What do you call the most evil cricket player in the world?
A wicket, wicket man.

In which sport do you put your left stick in, your left stick out, in, out, in, out, shake it all about?
The hockey-cokey.

What did one rugby player say to the other?
'You're really bringing me down, man.'

Rugby player: I can't seem to get the ball over the line.
Rugby coach: Try, Peter, try!

Why did the footballer foul another player? He did it for kicks.

Why did the chicken get sent off the pitch?
For fowl play.

Why is a football like a fish? They both get caught by a net.

Football coach 1: My team can jump higher than a crossbar.
Football coach 2: No, they can't, crossbars can't jump!

Why did the runner get a stitch? Because the race was sew long.

Running team: Coach, why are you lighting a fire?
Coach: I'm trying to get you lot warmed up.

Why are canoeists nosy?
They keep sticking their oar in.

What do you call the person who holds the record for eating the most?
The world chomp-ion.

SICK NOTES

Deer teecher

James is sik tooday and he wont be kuming to skool until after the speling test.
from

My mum x

Dear Mr Williams

Harry has picked up a nasty bug. I've asked him to put it back in the garden where it belongs but he won't listen to me.

Yours truly

Mrs Worrywarts

Dear Mr Williams

Rees is off school because some big angry red spots have appeared. We've calmed them down a bit but they're still fairly annoyed about something. Hopefully, we'll work it out soon.

From

Mr and Mrs Onable

Dear Mr Williams

Raphael fell off a neighbour's tree while trying to steal the apples and, as a result, has broken his leg. And if he ever tries it again I'll be breaking the other one, too.

Yours truly

Mr N. Gree

MUSICAL ¢ MAYHEM

IS THAT THE SOUND OF MUSIC WE HEAR OR IS IT THE SCHOOL CAT AGAIN?

Why were the music class eating cheese sandwiches?
They were out of tuna.

Where's the piano teacher?
He's gone for a little tinkle.

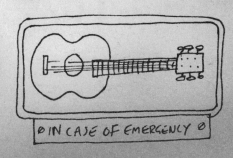

IN CASE OF EMERGENCY

Why did the police turn up at guitar class?
The teacher used the emergency chord.

What are a
cat's favourite
instruments?
Purr-cussion.

What's red,
sticky and gets
shaken a lot?
A jambourine.

What is Satan's
favourite
instrument?
Sin-bals.

Why is a drum kit like a bad
football team?
They both get beaten a lot.

Why is the school orchestra so
smelly?
They have a large wind section.

Why did the burglar come to the music class? He wanted his Lute (Loot).

What did one violin say to the other? 'Chin up!'

Where can you buy cheap recorders? At the descant shop.

How do you know if the music teacher's in a bad mood? She gets a bit crotchet-y.

How do you know if she's upset? Her voice goes all quaver-y.

50% OFF!

YOU KNOW YOUR SCHOOL'S REALLY STUPID WHEN . . .

The teachers are better at doing handstands than the pupils.

The whole of Wednesday is devoted to Latin American ballroom dancing.

ALL the pupils have the words 'Left' and 'right' stamped on their shoes.

Your school uniform is lime-green shorts and a stripy orange vest — and that's just for winter.

You ask your teacher when the SATs are and he says he's never heard of them.

The headmistress lets you call her Brenda, even though her name's Winifred.

The mums and dads come to the parents' evening in fancy dress.

If you want to go to the toilet you have to put your hand up and say 'Permission to do a poo, Sir.'

The teachers do the registers in anagrams. Ana Richards is now known as 'A Rancid Rash'.

The school song, which is sung every morning in assembly, is the one that starts 'O Pizza Hut, O Pizza Hut . . .'

GHASTLY GARMENTS

SCHOOL UNIFORMS. WE ALL HAVE TO WEAR THEM — AND WE ALL HATE THEM.

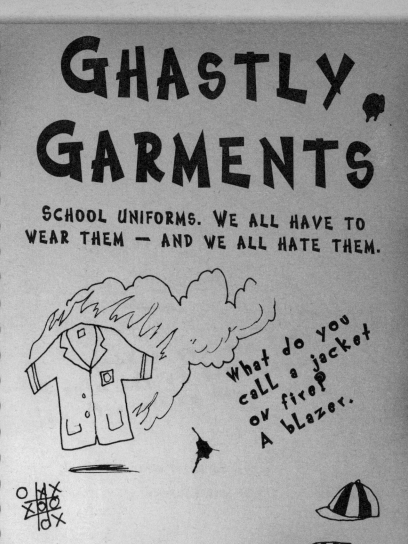

What do you call a jacket on fire?
A blazer.

What did the tie say to the hat?
'You go on a head while I hang around.'

What did one smelly sock say to the other?
'Are you stinking what I'm stinking?'

What did one school jumper say to the other? 'Don't get shirty with me!'

What do sheep wear to school?
Their ewe-niforms.

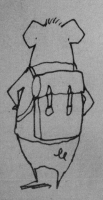

Where does a pig keep his school books? In his mucksack.

What did the trousers say
to the annoying dog?
'Are you pulling my leg?'

Where's the best
place to buy your
uniform?
Tieland.

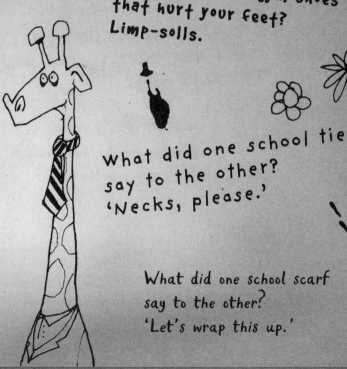

What do you call gym shoes
that hurt your feet?
Limp-solls.

What did one school tie
say to the other?
'Necks, please.'

What did one school scarf
say to the other?
'Let's wrap this up.'

*HOORAY FOR THE HOLIDAYS

TERM HAS ENDED, THE HOLIDAYS HAVE BEGUN, CHUCK OUT YOUR SCHOOL BAG AND HAVE SOME FUN!

Which sun lotion do maths teachers use? The one with the highest factor.

Why did the Egyptian mummy go to the beach? To unwind a little.

What were the lollies doing
in the freezer cabinet?
Just chillin'.

What kind of ice cream
jumps out and shouts 'Boo!'
Shocklate flavour.

What do witches use to
stop getting sunburnt?
Suntan potion.

What did the
tongue say to
the ice cream?
'I'll soon lick
you into shape.'

CRAB RANK

TAXI

What lives in
the sea and
takes you
where you
want to go?
A taxi-crab.

Why is seafood
good for you?
Because it gives
you mussels.

How did the popstar keep
cool on the beach?
She was surrounded by fans.

What folds up and goes
'Quack, quack'?
A duckchair.

How do you know if
someone's just eaten seafood?
They've got clam-my hands.

Where can you find
alligators on a beach?
In a croc-pool.

What did the mummy wave
say to the little wave?
'Time to tide-y up!'

Where do you keep
your holiday money?
In a sandbank.

Boy: Mum, Mum, put those boxes
of raisins away!

Mum: Why?

Boy: Because that sign says:
'Beware of dangerous currents'.

Why don't
mermaids
have
straight
hair?
Because
the sea
makes it
wave-y.

OH NO, NOT 'BACK TO SCHOOL'!

YOU KNOW THE SCORE. NO SOONER HAVE YOU BROKEN UP FOR THE SUMMER HOLIDAYS THAN YOU'RE BEING TOLD TO GET BACK IN THE CLASSROOM AGAIN. AND THAT MEANS IT'S TIME FOR THE DREADED 'BACK TO SCHOOL' SHOPPING TRIP!

What you really want is . . .
a new mobile phone with
polyphonic ringtone and
picture messaging.
What you actually get is
. . . a notebook and pencil.

What you really want is . . . a mountain bike with semi-slick tyres and adjustable alloy leg suspension.

GET TO SCHOOL KIT

CONTENTS: 1 PAIR OF SHOES

What you actually get is . . . told to walk to school, lazy.

What you really want is . . . to take advantage of that fantastic offer for 3 for 2 DVDs.

What you actually get is . . . to take advantage of that fantastic offer for 3 for 2 pairs of school socks.

What you really want is . . . a three-day trip to a theme park to try out the new 'Deathrider' rollercoaster.

What you actually get is . . . a three-hour trip to a department store to try out new school blazers.

What you really want is . . . a hilariously funny collection of joke books, very similar to the one you're now holding in your hand.

What you actually get is . . . a seriously unfunny collection of Learn-at-Home maths textbooks.

MATHS PART 1

PART 2

PART 4

What you really want is . . . brand-new air-cushioned trainers with holographic stripes.

What you actually get is . . . a brand-new school uniform that's a crime against fashion.

What you really want is . . . for the summer holidays to go on till Christmas.

What you actually get is . . . that sinking feeling when you remember you haven't even started your holiday project.

TEN INVENTIONS THAT WOULD MAKE SCHOOL LIFE MUCH EASIER

A 'smart' school bag that comes to you when you whistle.

The ability instantly to beam yourself directly from your bedroom to the classroom.

Intelligent pens that come up with bright ideas as you write.

$2 + 2 =$

Obedient robot teachers whose sole existence is to serve you.

Self-cleaning PE kit.

Jet-powered trainers that give you that extra spurt of energy on the sports field.

An invisibility cloak for the next time you're hauled in to see the headmaster.

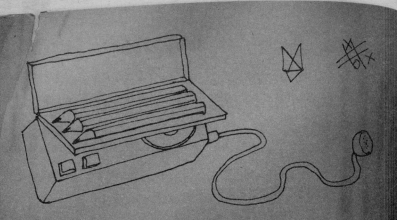

Miniature wireless DVD
players to conceal inside
your pencil case, for
particularly boring classes.

Homework that does
itself while you're
watching TV.

A tracking device that
tells you exactly where
any teacher is lurking,
at any time.

QUIZ – ARE YOU A SCHOOL FOOL OR A PLAYGROUND PRODIGY?

HOW MUCH DO YOU REALLY KNOW ABOUT SCHOOL? TEST YOUR UP-TO-THE-MINUTE KNOWLEDGE WITH OUR HIGHLY EDUCATIONAL QUIZ, APPROVED BY THE RECOGNIZED YET UNOFFICIAL BIG BOARD OF INTELLIGENT, SMART HEAD TEACHERS (OTHERWISE KNOWN AS R.U.B.B.I.S.H).

Teachers shout a lot because:

A. They love the sound of their own voices.

B. It's the only way they can get heard above the terrible noise their class is making.

C. They're just very angry people.

What does PSHE stand for?

A. Pupils are So Happy 'Ere.

B. People Say Headmaster's Evil.

C. Plimsolls Smelly, Hide Everyone.

A healthy lunchbox consists of:

A. Erm. Sandwiches?

B. A truckload of chips.

C. A family-sized bag of cheesy puffs, (the ones that make your mouth go bright orange) washed down with a few cans of fizzy drinks.

The most common excuse for not doing your homework is:

A. A dog ate it.

B. A cat ate it.

C. I ate it. (Well, I didn't have time for breakfast this morning.)

What is a ruler?

A. A long straight thing that helps you draw lines.

B. The head of a country, e.g. a king.

C. A power-crazed maniac who bosses everyone around, e.g. a teacher.

RESULTS

Mostly As
Congratulations! You passed with top grades. Your uncanny ability to guess the right answers with your eyes closed makes you the official classroom swot. Go, geeky!

Mostly Bs
A reasonable effort but could try harder. You need to listen more in class — did you hear me? YOU *NEED TO LISTEN MORE!!!!!!*

Mostly Cs
Oh dear. Do you ever go to school? You're right at the bottom of the class. As punishment, you have to write out one hundred times, 'I must try not to be so stupid.' What? You can't write . . .

AND
FINALLY...

'Knock, knock.'
'Who's there?'
'Gladys.'
'Gladys who?'
'Gladys it's the end of term!'